The Universal Individual Rights Project
A Worldwide Freedom Movement In A Book
A Blueprint For Peace, Prosperity And Freedom
A New System Of Rational Individualism
by
Kira Saoirse

About the Cover

We've found and chosen a new Universal Liberty Symbol for the Project!

Our first thoughts turned to the Statue of Liberty, but that's a specific symbol of one nation and we didn't want to give the impression that we were advocating imposing the political system of the United States on the rest of the world. This Project far transcends that, as you'll realize when you read it..

The 1933 gold Double Eagle.

It was banned in 1933 by Socialist President Franklin D. Roosevelt.

"Nearly half a million of the gold coins were minted in the U.S. in 1933 in the midst of the Great Depression but only 13 are known to exist today. The rest of the coins, featuring an eagle on one side and Liberty on the other, were melted down before they ever left the United States Mint, sacrificed as part of a strategy to remove America from the gold standard and stabilise the American economy." - The Daily Mail, February 9th, 2009.

We now know how well **that** worked out.

"Only one coin is legally in private hands, with all other 1933 Double Eagles remaining as property of the U.S. government, and the U.S. secret service pursues any newly discovered coins." - The Daily Mail, February 9th, 2009.

It's as rare as liberty itself, there are only 13 left in world and the only one privately owned is worth 7 million. And like liberty, they continue to be hunted by the U.S. government!

We think that this powerful symbol also epitomizes the philosophical concepts of the value of real money, that were put forth by Ayn Rand in "Atlas Shrugged"!

The Universal Individual Rights Project

A Worldwide Freedom Movement In A Book
A Blueprint For Peace, Prosperity And Freedom
A New System Of Rational Individualism
by
Kira Saoirse

Preface

It's become increasingly clear, in recent years, that the world now stands at the precipice of a disaster, the likes of which has never before been witnessed in history – a **Global Economic Collapse.** There's a distinct possibility that it could precipitate the end of any remaining vestiges of human freedom and sink humanity into an abyss of tyranny, perhaps for so long into the future that humanity would never know any hint of liberty in the same way again. This has become evident to me in recent years, and to anyone who honestly takes a look at what's going on, without the bias of any pre-existing agenda.

Governments all over the world have been becoming all-consuming – even the ones that previously weren't extremely destructive of liberty and individual economic prosperity.

We at the Universal Individual Rights Project think and conclude that these things can't be "fixed", that they're caused by systemic philosophical problems, that the systems themselves are the problems, and that only by changing them, can the world hope to avoid a truly horrible disaster.

What has forced-collectivism brought the world, and what is it likely to result in? This passage from "Anthem" gets right to the point of what we face:

"At first, man was enslaved by the gods. But he broke their chains. Then he was enslaved by the kings. But he broke their chains. He was enslaved by his birth, by his kin, by his race. But he broke their chains. He declared to all his brothers that a man has rights which neither god nor king nor other men can take away from him, no matter what their number, for his is the right of man, and there is no right on earth above this right. And he stood on the threshold of the freedom for which the blood of the centuries behind him had been spilled.

But then he gave up all he had won, and fell lower than his savage beginning.

What brought it to pass? What disaster took their reason away from men? What whip lashed them to their knees in shame and submission? The worship of the word "We."" --Ayn Rand, from the novella, "Anthem".

Dedication

This book is dedicated to two of my favorite heroes, the writer and philosopher Alisa Zinov'yevna Rosenbaum, better known to us by her pen name "Ayn Rand", and to my favorite of the American Revolutionary period, one of the founders of the United States, Thomas Jefferson.

Rand grew up in the Stalinist Soviet Union (Her novel, *"We The Living"*.) and witnessed first-hand, the utterly devastating effects of the very worst that forced-collectivism can become. It is estimated that over two hundred million people were killed in the 20th century alone, by various forms of forced-collectivism.

She admired the thoughts and writings of Thomas Jefferson and took his ideas, along with her own, to a whole new, more modern, articulate and evolved level. For these reasons, many forced-collectivists hate her works with a dark passion, lie about her and smear her relentlessly. Those are their ways and strategies.

"Any means to an end." - Saul Alinsky, Rules for Radicals.

Rand expressed the opposite of that, with her philosophy of Objectivism. Note: For those not yet familiar, when I refer to the terms "Objectivist" or "Objectivism" in this book, I'm referring to the philosophy of Ayn Rand.

"My philosophy, in essence, is the concept of man as a heroic being, with his own happiness as the moral purpose of his life, with productive achievement as his noblest activity, and reason as his only absolute."
   – *Ayn Rand*

And last but not least, to Jennifer S. Brookstone, my life-long best friend, who helped proof read the book.

Introduction

In some dark days and nights of the winter of 2010, when time was plentiful and work was scarce, I was pondering about what "rights" are. Here in the United States, we've had a unique role in history, being one of the few nations in the world that not only recognized rights since its founding, but recognized them as not being granted as privileges to us, by governments. They were deemed as belonging to us as human beings – human rights. At the time, I was thinking of our Bill of Rights. If we, as Americans, had inalienable rights, as human beings, then why didn't the rest of the world?

It was along these lines of thought that I began to entertain the idea, of not only modernizing our Bill of Rights and explaining to the rest of the world why everyone has them, every bit as much as we Americans do. As that process evolved, I even thought of elaborating upon them, more than our Bill of Rights had. This book is the product of that thinking.

So, What Are Rights?

We live in a world where definitions of rights have been twisted by such a long and dreary history of forced-collectivism, that probably most people alive now confuse rights with <u>entitlements</u>. So what are rightfully rights? For some better definitions, I turned not only to the dictionary, but to the Objectivist philosophy of Ayn Rand.

As a prerequisite, it must be pointed out that there are no such things as "collective rights", in fact that phrase is an oxymoron – a contradiction. The American system of government recognized the fact that **rights** could only rightfully belong to **individuals** and that **powers** were bestowed by the People upon **governments**. This is an absolutely **crucial** distinction. Therefore, no government has **ever** had the "**right** to keep and bear arms". Only individual **People** have ever had that right, and governments are given the **power** to bear arms by the People, providing that those governments are legitimate, and not forms of tyranny. This is clearly illustrated, as follows.

First, the dictionary: "hu/Eman rights/E,

fundamental rights, esp. those believed to belong to an individual and in whose exercise a government may not interfere, as the rights to speak*, associate, work, etc." [1785-95] " · Dictionary.com Unabridged · Based on the Random House Dictionary, © Random House, Inc. 2011.

* Keep and bear arms, etc.
Example: The *Right to Keep and Bear Arms* (what many of us Americans refer to as "RKBA") is a human right.

So what are rights?

"A "right" is a moral principle defining and sanctioning a man's freedom of action in a social context. There is only one fundamental right (all the others are its consequences or corollaries): a man's right to his own life. Life is a process of self-sustaining and self-generated action; the right to life means the right to engage in self-sustaining and self-generated action— which means: the freedom to take all the actions required by the nature of a rational being for the support, the furtherance, the fulfillment and the enjoyment of his own life. (Such is the meaning of the right to life, liberty and the pursuit of happiness.)

The concept of a "right" pertains only to action - specifically, to freedom of action. It means freedom from physical compulsion, coercion or interference by other men.

Thus, for every individual, a right is the moral sanction of a positive - of his freedom to act on his own judgment, for his own goals, by his own voluntary, uncoerced choice.

As to his neighbors, his rights impose no obligations on them except of a negative kind: to abstain from violating his rights.

The right to life is the source of all rights—and the right to property is their only implementation. Without property rights, no other rights are possible. Since man has to sustain his life by his own effort, the man who has no right to the product of his effort has no means to sustain his life. The man who produces while others dispose of his product, is a slave.

Bear in mind that the right to property is a right to action, like all the others: it is not the right to an object, but to the action and the consequences of producing or earning that object. It is not a guarantee that a man will earn any property, but only a guarantee that he will own it if he earns it. It is the right to gain, to keep, to use and to dispose of material values." -- Ayn Rand

"Any alleged "right" of one man, which necessitates the violation of the rights of another, is not and cannot be a right. No man can have a right to impose an unchosen obligation, an unrewarded duty or an involuntary servitude on another man. There can be no such thing as "the right to enslave". -- Ayn Rand

It's beyond the scope of this book, but if you're interested in a more thorough explanation of the proper and precise **derivation** of rights, I highly recommend the essay:

"**Libertarianism vs. Radical Capitalism**", by **Craig Biddle**, of **The Objective Standard**. If you have access to the internet, it should be readily available online.

It's an excellent explanation of why we have rights, based on Objectivist philosophy, without having to "reinvent the wheel" by going into that much detail in this book.

If you're interested in a very thorough examination of what rights are and how they're solidly derived, I highly recommend the following books and sources of the works of Ayn Rand:

Objectivism is explained in "What Is Objectivism", at: http://www.atlassociety.org/what_is_objectivism

I also recommend reading these books by Ayn Rand, to get the full depth of her philosophy:

"Atlas Shrugged"
"The Virtue of Selfishness"
"Anthem"
"Philosophy: Who Needs It"
(See her speech at West Point, 1974:
http://fare.tunes.org/liberty/library/pwni.html)
"Capitalism: The Unknown Ideal"
"For the New Intellectual"

As I read Rand's books, I'd highlight the most amazing and powerful passages with a yellow highlight marker, but I soon found that I was highlighting very large portions of each book.

"Textbook of Americanism" which is free online: http://www.hartford-hwp.com/archives/10/091.html is also excellent - everyone should read it!

I fully understand that various people derive rights in their own minds, though various means. Some derive them via religion, and some through philosophy, as I do. There are many paths up a mountain. This doesn't mean that rights are somehow subjective. As Ayn Rand pointed out, words have objective meanings and rights can be objectively defined, it's just that many people arrive at similar understandings of rights, without the solid derivation processes and explanations that Rand's philosophy provides. And that's OK, but it leaves a weakness when it comes to defending your rights against very powerful forces that will argue that you don't really have them.

But I really think that there is no more thorough and solid an explanation of how they're rightfully derived, than **Ayn Rand's philosophy of Objectivism.** It can stand up to any forced-collectivist arguments without breaking down, to the point where your opponent will eventually resort to ad hominem (personal) attacks and smears, at which point you know you've won.

That being said, it's the purpose of this book, to work towards uniting all of those in the world, who favor liberty and individual rights, whether or not they have the philosophical bedrock that I think Objectivism offers. I think that if we wait for everyone to arrive at the same understanding that I think Objectivists have, it could prove fatal to human liberty.

This book is an attempt to encourage and promote individual rights along the lines of that philosophy, in a condensed form, "in a nutshell", so to speak, so that almost anyone in the world can grasp it.

It's an attempt to apply the philosophy of Objectivism towards a universal political system that can ensure liberty, peace and prosperity for all the people of the world who are willing to work for it.

But is it already too late?

So then we face the question of whether it is already too late to pull the world back from the brink of the aforementioned abyss, and save - even expand and promote human liberty? Call me an eternal optimist - I think that it can be done. But only with a massive educational effort, as to the principles of liberty, and a philosophy that matches and promotes them in the world. That was the main reason that this book was written - to be sort of a beam of light towards liberty.

It does not take a majority to prevail... but rather an irate, tireless minority, keen on setting brush fires of freedom in the minds of men." - Samuel Adams

"La libertad no es negotiable."
(Liberty is not negotiable.)
– Jose Marti, Cuban patriot

"I know... it sounds bad. But you have to understand something: it's times like these, when long standing patterns are disrupted that things become more fluid. That's when a small group of people, or even a single individual, can change the course of history." - The TV series "Dark Matter, on SyFy.

What It's About and What It's Not

This book isn't about national politics in the United States; Democrats versus Republicans, "left" versus "right", liberals versus conservatives, etc. It's about the essential forces that have been at work in philosophy and politics, around the world, since people first organized themselves into societies. Looking at the following chart, the essence of these things has been distilled into a vertical scale, to avoid the left versus right analogy. It's a continuum that I call **forced-collectivism versus voluntary collectivism** – the latter regions being where individual rights reign. That's what the discussion needs to be about, if we're to avoid global catastrophe, war, misery, poverty and the loss of individual rights and true human dignity.

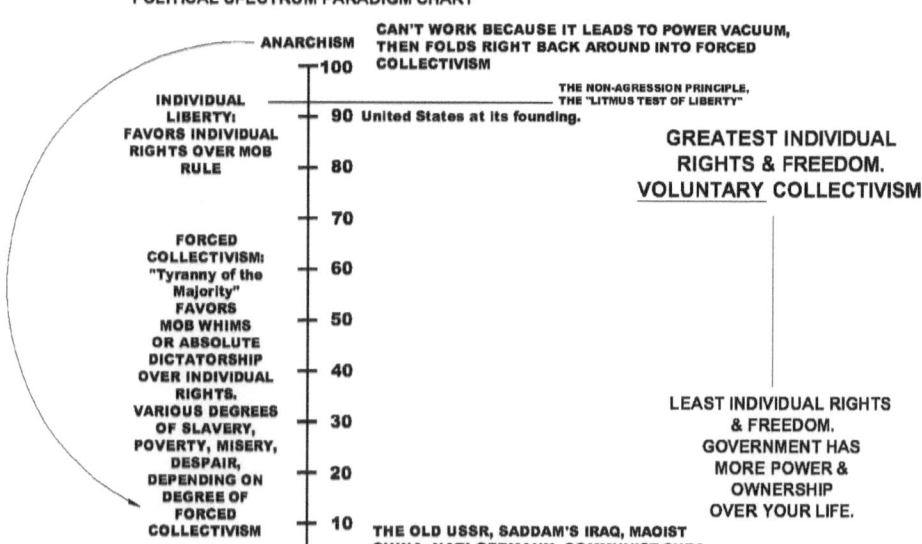

INDIVIDUAL RIGHTS VS FORCED COLLECTIVISM
RELATIVE PERCENTAGE OF FREEDOM
POLITICAL SPECTRUM PARADIGM CHART

ANARCHISM

CAN'T WORK BECAUSE IT LEADS TO POWER VACUUM, THEN FOLDS RIGHT BACK AROUND INTO FORCED COLLECTIVISM

100

THE NON-AGRESSION PRINCIPLE, THE "LITMUS TEST OF LIBERTY"

INDIVIDUAL LIBERTY: FAVORS INDIVIDUAL RIGHTS OVER MOB RULE

90 United States at its founding.

80

GREATEST INDIVIDUAL RIGHTS & FREEDOM. VOLUNTARY COLLECTIVISM.

70

FORCED COLLECTIVISM: "Tyranny of the Majority" FAVORS MOB WHIMS OR ABSOLUTE DICTATORSHIP OVER INDIVIDUAL RIGHTS. VARIOUS DEGREES OF SLAVERY, POVERTY, MISERY, DESPAIR, DEPENDING ON DEGREE OF FORCED COLLECTIVISM

60

50

40

30

20

10

LEAST INDIVIDUAL RIGHTS & FREEDOM. GOVERNMENT HAS MORE POWER & OWNERSHIP OVER YOUR LIFE.

THE OLD USSR, SADDAM'S IRAQ, MAOIST CHINA, NAZI GERMANY, COMMUNIST CUBA, NORTH KOREA

0

TOTALITARIAN

Why the term *"forced-collectivism"*?

I think that the term *"Forced-collectivism"* is the best description for societies that are based in vague notions such as "social contract" theory. "Social contract" theory amounts to some mob (forced-collective) of people coming along and saying; If you live in our society (our forced-collective), you must agree to live the way that **we** tell you to, and pay a tribute of a certain percentage of your life to the collective, or you will be forced to comply.

There's a huge difference between that and voluntary relationships, or a voluntary collective – voluntary collectivism. The latter is freedom, the former can be compared to an organized crime syndicate, in which the criminal organization comes to a person or business and says; "You're on our turf. You must pay us tribute or we will kill you". The only difference between that and a government is that, by definition, what the government does is legal. (They defined it that way.) But *"what's right isn't always legal and what's legal isn't always right"*.

Voluntary collectives are fine, and in this book I will attempt to explain why <u>forced</u> collectives are the bane of peace, prosperity and freedom. They always have been, and they always will be.

When socialist-leaning people find out that I'm an Objectivist - an individual rights advocate, the most frequent comment is something like; "Well you don't believe in society", "You don't want any government", or; "You're an anarchist!". This is simply not true. I've lived in society all of my life. I love living in society. It's just that I've recently begun to identify the differences between **free** societies and societies that have varying degrees of **slavery**.

The next most common comment is something like; "Well you don't have any sympathy or compassion for your fellow human beings who are less fortunate than you are, and are in "need". You must not believe in charity."

I absolutely do, and support charities all the time. I just discern the differences between **true charity, which is giving of one's own free will, "from the heart"**, and **forced "charity" which isn't really charity at all, for the very reason that it's forced.** If someone has to threaten you with force, to pay taxes, that they redistribute according to their whims, to those who they feel "need" them (and very often, just to their friends and cronies), is that "charity"?

No.

Voluntary collectives and (consensual) relationships are fine, and are the very essence of freedom. The free market teems with them: Private businesses, clubs, co-ops, jobs, religious or social organizations), etc.

The essence is that these are **voluntary collectives**, based on voluntary (**consensual**) agreements and relationships that people can always opt out of, if their circumstances change, or they simply change their minds. **That's freedom.**

Any **contracts** made voluntarily are perfectly enforceable in the courts because of that. They're agreements between two or more consenting adult parties.

But if someone holds a gun to your head and tells you to sign something, it's done under duress and freedom-loving people will not recognize that as a valid contract. It might be valid in forced-collectivist nations, dictatorships and under various forms of organized criminal rule. **But if it's not acceptable when a criminal mob does it, how does it somehow become acceptable when a government does it?**

There's a great big flaw to the premise that individuals are too lazy, stupid, incompetent or evil to run their own lives, without having them dictated by the collective. Yet **somehow** forced-collectives are competent to do so.

"Sometimes it is said that man cannot be trusted with the government of himself. Can he, then, be trusted with the government of others? Or have we found angels in the forms of kings to govern him? Let history answer this question." -- Thomas Jefferson, First Inaugural Address.

And that's not all. In his book *"People of The Lie"*, M. Scott Peck also explained the nature of *"group evil"*. People do things in groups that they would never dare to do as individuals. (Examples are "lynch mobs", dictatorships and forced-collectivist legislatures.) People gain courage from mobs, that they wouldn't normally have, to do anything ranging from making it illegal to spit on the sidewalk, to committing genocide. Mobs protect their anonymity and shield them from the usual and otherwise direct and immediate consequences of their actions. This is also often referred to as "initiating force by proxy". The legislator doesn't have to have the nerve or the courage to directly initiate physical force against people, they send the police or military to do it.

Can one individual make a difference in this world?

The various flavors of forced-collectivists tell us, "no". They have reasons for wanting you to believe that, usually involving various combinations of money, control and power, for themselves, and their friends in their own favorite interest groups. Their philosophy also holds that individuals are too *lazy, stupid, incompetent or evil* to run their own lives, without having everything dictated to them by the forced collective.

It's not true.

"Contradictions do not exist. Whenever you think that you are facing a contradiction, check your premises. You will find that one of them is wrong." - Francisco D'Anconia, from "Atlas Shrugged" by Ayn Rand.

One person can absolutely make a difference, so never let anyone convince you otherwise.

The answer is: "**Yes, I can!**".

Throughout human history, individuals have made profound differences in this world; inventors, philosophers, creators, scientists, the list is enormous. Even just the average person.

The author of this book started out as a '60's liberal, and due to some very extraordinary life experiences, began a radical transformation of thought and the most fundamental philosophy in the early '90's, which continues to this day.

The Universal Individual Rights Project was originated and developed by an individual.

This Project started with the Bill of Rights of the United States, which is not copyrighted after these two plus centuries. That was my starting point.

Admittedly, a few parts were modernized, and I attempted to clarify their meaning, in more modern terms. Like the quotes I so liberally like to use, why reinvent the wheel?

I'm only human and far from perfect. No one who knows about my life could ever accuse me of that. I don't have any plans to run for President. I've done my own share of screwing up my life, and fortunately survived so far, despite it.

I grew up as a '60's "moderate" liberal (closer to what people think of as a pre-Marxist "classic liberal") who had always been interested, in certain respects, in individual rights.

Years ago, I used to express it as; "People should be able to live the way they want, as long as they don't infringe the equal rights of others." But that later proved to be too vague.

I had always been involved in the advocacy and defense of "RKBA" - the "Right to Keep And Bear Arms" movement, here in the United States, which I always considered to be an extension of the fundamental "natural right" to self defense – and an also-fundamental right to own, keep and use the most modern means of self defense available.

That debate has been hotly raging since the 1960's in this country, and I could never understand why it was of very little apparent concern to the rest of the world. Something to do with Americans' heritage of something called "individual rights". Things that weren't bestowed on us by government, but were said to be inherent in our very nature and were most often suppressed and oppressed by governments.

"Liberty has never come from the government. Liberty has always come from the subjects of the government. The history of government is a history of resistance. The history of liberty is the history of the limitation of government, not the increase of it."
--Woodrow Wilson (Of all people!)

I've since found out just how ironic that quote was, coming from whom it did - essentially a Fabian Progressive Socialist, but the essence of it stands as true.

So we were engaged in this fierce debate during those years, about whether the RKBA was an individual right or a "collective right" as the more forced-collectivist elements of our society claimed.

As I stated earlier, I came to the conclusion that "rights" cannot be had by governments, at all.

So upon further thinking, reading of our Constitution and listening to constitutional scholars, I realized that only individuals can have <u>rights</u>.

Governments can only have <u>powers</u> that are granted to them by "The People" and don't infringe individual rights of the people, and they should have few of those, our actual Constitution being an interesting example of that.

So now when I see politicians orating about the "government having the right" to do this or that, I can't help but wonder about how much they've thought out the very basis of our system of government, studied the Constitution, or about what their <u>real</u> agenda may be.

Our Supreme Court has since ruled fairly decisively on the issue, based on these things and our history, that **the right to keep and bear arms is an individual right.**

It was this budding realization about human (individual) rights that got me thinking about the Bill of Rights of the United States, also known as the first ten Amendments of our Constitution.

With our Second Amendment, the more radical forced-collectivists were working very hard to misinterpret that human right out of existence, through inveigling and obfuscation.

"...this particular right is threatened with misinterpretation to the point of meaninglessness... this is a far easier method of elimination than amendment, being much quicker and not requiring the same rigid consensus and forthright discussion of it's constitutional relevancy." - To Keep And Bear Arms, By Dr. Joyce Malcolm

I was later to find out that this was a very standard tactic of the "Progressive" (Meaning slowly "progressing" towards socialism.) movement, in a century-long effort to do away with our entire Constitution. Look into the Fabian Society – the roots of the modern Progressive movement. Some people will scoff at this and tell you that they existed years ago, but they still exist. Tony Blair and Gordon Brown are said to be among the most prominent modern members. Hillary Clinton is a self-described "Progressive" Socialist:

"I prefer the word progressive, which has a real American meaning, going back to the progressive era at the beginning of the 20th Century. I consider myself a modern progressive." - Hillary Clinton, July 23, 2007.

"...has a real American meaning"? The Fabian Progressive Socialists originated at the London School of Economics in the late 19th century.

Her words were probably not understood by the large body of plain everyday liberals, but it was code language, to those in her audience who understand **exactly** what **Fabian Progressive Socialism** is.

One of the things that helped the Progressive movement in their efforts, was the language of our Constitution and Bill of Rights, which was after all, over two hundred years old.

"Preamble

We the people of the United States, in order to form a more perfect union, establish justice, insure domestic tranquility, provide for the common defence, **promote the general welfare**, and secure the blessings of liberty to ourselves and our posterity, do ordain and establish this Constitution for the United States of America."

They've long held that this was an open invitation to **promote a welfare nanny state**, but it doesn't say "provide the general welfare", as in class warfare and redistribution of wealth, it says "promote", meaning to **encourage.**

And it doesn't say anything about promoting everyone's welfare in particular, just the welfare of the country in general.

So I began thinking along the lines of modernizing our Second Amendment, so there could be no room for doubt about what the founders intended. But they said it in language that would leave so much room for disingenuous misinterpretation in the following centuries.

"QUESTION AUTHORITY" - **Libertarian bumper sticker.**

Along the path of this thought process, I also started questioning why the principles of our Second Amendment wouldn't be just as valid for all the people of the world, not just for those of us in the United States. I quickly found that the forced-collectivist factions in the rest of the world, had already made such radical advances in conditioning peoples' ways of thinking and turning them docile, that very few people outside of the United States would even imagine such a thing anymore.

Asserting an individual right to self defense?

It was as if assertion of self-ownership had been bred out of most people outside of the United States and they had little, if any, concept of **individual rights**. Sometimes, and in some other parts of the world (even in the United States), they don't even grasp the concept of private property anymore.

Yet the reasoning behind the concept of the true definition of human (individual) rights holds true. Like the late Lewis Van Dercar, an artist I used to know in Florida, liked to teach people:

"Truth stands up to questioning. You can question it all you want and it won't break down."

Therefore, if our Constitution holds our rights as inalienable and our Second Amendment was a true individual human right, how could it **not** be just as much a human right for everyone else in the world, as for those of us here in the United States?

Answer: **It must be.**

Even if not **recognized** as such, by the governments and many of the people in those places!

Refusal to recognize a true human right, or ignorance of it, doesn't mean that it doesn't exist.

It only means that large numbers of people haven't worked through the thought processes, to recognize their **rightful human rights,** and that those in their governments are either similarly unaware, and/or knowingly tyrants.

Then the thought process that led to that realization about our Second Amendment evolved a little more. If our Second Amendment was just as valid and applicable an inalienable human right, applying to the people in the rest of the world, as it is to those of us in the United States, then why wouldn't our entire Bill of Rights be just as valid and applicable?

Answer: It is.

So, I thought;

How could we offer our Bill of Rights to the people of the rest of the world, and how could we help educate and awaken them to the facts that they too have these rights, and that their rights are philosophically provable?

Part of the challenge went back to that two hundred plus year- old language. If Progressives in our country could play games with it and try to inveigle and obfuscate it out of existence, how would people in the rest of the world be able to easily and clearly understand it?

So this became a learning and understanding process, a process of questioning, clarifying, and distilling the very essences of these things. I had to think, not only of how the founders intended our rights to be understood when they wrote them, but of how to put them into a modern context of their pure essences and distill them down, so that modern people could easily understand them and they would be understood as inalienable and undeniable.

Was anything left out? Was anything less relevant today, or could it be put in more modern and relevant terms?

Then there was the derivation process. We have a major divide in the world, between large numbers of theists, who believe that their rights (if any) derive from their deity, and large numbers of atheists, who would need another path by which to understand such derivation.

Large numbers of people among the world's population, after all, are atheists due to the influences and oppression of socialism and communism. Others come by it, from science and/or philosophy.

So I had to *attempt* to explain the derivation of *inalienable human rights*, to people of both persuasions, in terms that were non-offensive, yet using pathways that could merge into the same realizations, with the same conclusions. I think that the chart you see in this book can accomplish that.

But if you want the ideal path to the derivation of rights, I still urge you to read the novels of Ayn Rand, and her books and materials, with which she founded the philosophy of Objectivism. **I haven't found anything that I can agree with more than that, it's rock solid.**

The reason that I'm elaborating all of these things here, is that we don't have the time for enough people in the world, to read and absorb her writings, in time to pull the world back from the impending abyss. And I wanted to frame these things in more universal and simplified terms, that almost anyone and everyone in the world could understand and relate to, until such time as Objectivism can be propagated more widely.

As this thought process evolved over the years, since about the mid-'90's, these ideas became distilled and purified into a form that I began to realize could be of great value towards understanding and explaining our rights, and why everyone in the world could rightfully claim them for themselves.

With all the non-rightful "entitlements"* in the world today, being thought of by so many people as "rights", human (individual) rights are the _**only**_ type of truly rightful rights.

* People with liberal/socialist leanings have asked me about the "U.N. Declaration of Human Rights", but that's really more of a declaration of socialist entitlements, and I think, a pretty shameful document. It would destroy the world, if it was ever implemented.

"A Bill Of Rights is what the people are entitled to against every government on earth, general or particular, and what no just government should refuse, or rest on inference." -Thomas Jefferson

Could Jefferson have been anticipating that some day the rest of the world might evolve to understand and accept these fundamental principles of liberty for themselves? That they should be extended and offered to everyone in the world, not just to Americans?

But along the way, I also began to realize that there were some very important fundamental things that didn't quite fit into a Bill of Rights, but were very necessary restrictions that "We The People" should place on our governments. We see so many signs of their necessity today, and of governments running amok, from not being _forced_ by "The People" to adhere to certain very basic rules that respect and recognize our individual human rights.

No, Not Anarchism

But also let me be very clear here. I am in no way any kind of an anarchist. I agree with Ayn Rand completely on that issue. I think that the fatal flaw with anarchism is that it causes a power vacuum, and soon thereafter, someone will step in and fill it. In the ensuing disorder, people will clamor for - guess what – forced-collectivism, to protect them.

"In the end they will lay their freedom at our feet, and say to us, "Make us your slaves, but feed us."" - Dostoevsky

Even in Somalia for example, a country that has long been held out by forced-collectivists as an example of "anarchy", and of why too much freedom can't work, they don't really have true anarchy.

I say this from the experience of spending many hours in discussions years ago, with a bona fide philosophical anarchist, who was very well-read on the subject and really knew it.

In the theoretical working anarchist society, everyone would just cooperate and be free at the same time, no longer needing any government.

In Somalia they have multitudes of power groups, many of them involving radical Islam, and various war lords and pirates. More like modern expressions of feudalism.

It illustrates my point exactly, that because it creates a power vacuum, anarchy wraps right back around into some form of forced-collectivism. It cannot remain self sustaining, at **least** until humans evolve to the point where they get along so well, and understand the principles of freedom so well, that they no longer need any government.

How long will that take? Hundreds of more years? Thousands?

This country was never in a true state of anarchy, but it came close at the beginning. Our founders eventually managed to find a sweet spot that lead to a great deal of freedom, peace and prosperity, for as long as it was observed – small government combined with individual rights (freedom), including private property ownership and free markets.

As soon as people started neglecting those things and/or forgetting them, things started deteriorating.

And by the same token, I think the opposite of anarchy must be avoided at all costs too – totalitarianism. In our worst nightmare scenario lies the dreaded *"One World Government"* - what the conspiracy theorists talk about as the *"New World Order"*. *Recently* we've discovered that it wasn't a "theory" at all, it's right out there in the open in the words and writings of the Progressive Socialist movement that started after Karl Marx, and has been working towards that goal ever since, under various labels. (see *"Fabian Socialism"*)

George Soros recently used the term "a new world order", as being a desirable thing, with the United States losing its power and China taking over as super power.

""I think you need a new world order, that China has to be part of the process of creating it and they have to buy in, they have to own it in the same way as the United States owns...the current order", said (George) Soros, adding that the G20 was a move in this direction."

China in recent years, has been a country that has also discovered that Communism doesn't work - that if you take all the fleece from the sheep, they die in the winter cold. It's now a country that has discovered a sweet spot (for the rulers) of forced-collectivism, where they allow people to keep some of what they earn (the fleece of the sheep) and take the rest (partial economic freedom), while retaining totalitarian social control.

When President Clinton visited China, I was really wondering if he wasn't discussing exactly this, with them. Whether he, as a Progressive, was agreeing that both nations could "meet in the middle" and have societies that were economically free enough to be sustainable for taxation (fleecing) while meeting in the middle with social controls that would keep the Communists in power.

Yet, even more recently, it seems like some factions in China have realized the great evolution that has started to come about, by reducing Communism, in favor of freer trade and markets, combined with greater individual liberty. In recent months, we've even seen Yaron Brook of the Ayn Rand Institute, traveling to China to give talks to people there.

But as far as any agenda towards a one-world government, I think that globalist socialists like George Soros, with his OSI (Open Society Institute) plans, understand it all too well, and I think they envision it on a global scale.

So I think that now, we stand on an imbalanced scale, with some very large and well-funded factions pushing for globalist socialism, and a small liberty faction, striking the sparks of freedom in those who are ready to listen.

So let me be perfectly clear about this. This Project is the opposite of globalist socialism, or any form of globalism. It's absolutely not an attempt to form a "One World Government", "New World Order", or any of that.

It's an attempt to help educate people about the essential aspects of individual liberty, and what things they can rightfully demand of governments all around the world. And if said governments refuse them these individual rights, and constitutional demands that they stay within the confines of an inalienable individual rights-based Constitution and Bill of Rights, those governments can be thought of as tyrannies, to the extent that they deny these rights and practices to "The People".

It would be wonderful to see an "open society" some day, and a "world without borders", but not as a globalist one-world-government tyranny that taxed everyone and ruled us globally.

All freedom would be permanently lost!

It would be wonderful to see it happen by large scale adoption of a Bill of Rights and Constitution, as outlined here, where we would no longer need borders because everyone was free! **Let's make it happen!**

Author's Note: Since the original writing of this Project in 2010, I've done much more reading about Objectivism – the philosophy of Ayn Rand. It's been an amazing experience and I now think that it's the only philosophy that I've ever encountered, that I can agree with 100%.

This Project is an attempt to extend the American Revolution universally, while modernizing it, elaborating on it and removing the mechanisms that eventually defeated the liberty that it brought the United States and the world.

"...what the people are entitled to against every government on earth, general or particular, and what no just government should refuse, or rest on inference."

The additional things that people should rightfully demand from government, yet are not exactly "human (individual) rights", are better described as the basis for a Constitution of those articles. Yet in this unique case, it is not a Constitution that **forms** a government, but a Constitution of things that individual people the world over can rightfully demand, as **rightful restrictions on all governments.**

I've recently decided to describe that part of the concept as **"C.O.P.E."** - **"Constitution Of the People of Earth"**, and that The Universal Individual Rights Project should be spelled out first and foremost before it, so as to leave absolutely no doubts about what "We The People", as individuals who demand ownership of our own lives, are demanding of every government in the world.

Then the Bill of Rights should be followed by strong constitutional practices – things that The People should rightfully demand that all governments do, to ensure their peace, prosperity and freedom.

This little book is only a beginning, but I think that a beginning is what's needed.

"There's nothing as powerful as an idea that's time has come", and this is that time, if there ever was one in human history.

I think that we now face some *very* rough times, and they will either culminate in the destruction of society as we've known it (Read the little-known novella, *"Anthem"*, by Ayn Rand.) , or in the dawning of a new era of freedom, peace and prosperity, which is absolutely possible if people understand and apply the concepts in this book.

This book has been kept small, on purpose. The Constitution of the United States is small, but very concise and powerful. **When followed and enforced by the people on their governments**, it has led to peace, freedom and prosperity that has been unmatched in the world before it.

"The Constitution is either a <u>superior, paramount law</u>, unchangeable by ordinary means, or it is on a level with ordinary legislative acts and, like other acts, is alterable when the legislature shall please to alter it. If the former part of the alternative be true, then a legislative act contrary to the Constitution is not law; if the latter part be true, then written constitutions are absurd attempts, on the part of the people, to limit a power in its own nature illimitable." Thus, the Constitution is either The Supreme Law of the Land, superceding all other laws, or the Constitution is a worthless piece of paper. If the latter, government can do as it pleases. If the former, tyrants have seized sovereignty illegally, it is the duty of the people to put them in their proper place in history. - Chief Justice of the Supreme Court, John Marshall – 1803

"Article VI.

2 This Constitution, and the laws of the United States which shall be made in pursuance thereof; and all treaties made or which shall be made, under the authority of the United States, shall be the <u>supreme law of the land</u>; and the Judges in every State shall be bound thereby, any thing in the Constitution or laws of any State to the contrary notwithstanding."

Compared with that, we have a relative "tower of Babel" of laws that have been built by forced-collectivism **to control and rule us.** We have so many laws that even our own government here in the United States can't tell us how many there really are anymore, and they've been added to, by massive levels of bureaucracy that don't even answer to our lawmakers and in-effect, rule as mini-dictatorships, often along with "executive orders" that also amount to dictatorship.

It was with this in mind, that I wanted to keep this work small and relatively simple. Life doesn't have to be that complicated, but I think there are profound reasons why some people want it that way.

"Did you really think we want those laws observed?", said Dr. Ferris. We WANT them to be broken. You'd better get it straight that it's not a bunch of boy scouts you're up against.... We're after power and we mean it .... There's no way to rule innocent men. The only power any government has is the power to crack down on criminals. Well, when there aren't enough criminals one MAKES them. One declares so many things to be a crime that it becomes impossible for men to live without breaking laws. Who wants a nation of law abiding citizens? What's there in that for anyone? But just pass the kind of laws that can neither be observed nor enforced or objectively interpreted - and you create a nation of law-breakers-- and then you cash in on guilt. Now that's the system Mr. Reardon, that's the game, and once you understand it, you'll be much easier to deal with." – Ayn Rand, "Atlas Shrugged", 1957

The Fundamental Principles Underlying Liberty – Individual Rights, Must Be Non-Negotiable

"La libertad no es negotiable."
(Liberty isn't negotiable".)
- Jose Marti, Cuban patriot

It is said in the halls of power, that "politics is the art of compromise", but the fundamental underlying principles of liberty cannot be subject to compromise, or they cease to exist. **Rights that can be compromised can be compromised away.** In this respect, rights are like the hull of a manned spacecraft. In the movies, when they shout that "the hull has been compromised", that's a very bad thing, and people are about to die.

Human (individual) rights should not be subject to compromise (government regulation, or law-making that infringes them) otherwise they become privileges instead of rights. A right that can be compromised or "regulated" can be compromised away.

"A compromise is an adjustment of conflicting claims by mutual concessions. This means that both parties to a compromise have some valid claim and some value to offer each other. And this means that both parties agree upon some fundamental principle which serves as a base for their deal.

It is only in regard to concretes or particulars, implementing a mutually accepted basic principle, that one may compromise...

There can be no compromise between a property owner and a burglar; offering the burglar a single teaspoon of one's silverware would not be a compromise, but a total surrender - the recognition of his right to one's property. What value or concession did the burglar offer in return? And once the principle of unilateral concessions is accepted as the base of a relationship by both parties, it is only a matter of time before the burglar would seize the rest...

There can be no compromise between freedom and government controls; to accept "just a few controls" is to surrender the principle of inalienable individual rights and to substitute for it the principle of the government's unlimited arbitrary power, thus delivering oneself into gradual enslavement...

Today, however, when people speak of "compromise", what they mean is not a legitimate mutual concession or a trade, but precisely the betrayal of one's principles - the unilateral surrender to any groundless, irrational claim. The root of that doctrine is ethical subjectivism, which holds that a desire or whim is an irreducible moral primary, that every man is entitled to any desire he might feel like asserting, that all desires have equal moral validity, and that the only way men can get along together is by giving in to anything and "compromising" with anyone. It is not hard to see who would profit and who would lose by such a doctrine.

The immorality of this doctrine - and the reason why the term "compromise" implies, in today's general usage, an act of moral treason - lies in the fact that it requires men to accept ethical subjectivism as the basic principle superceding all principles in human relationships and to sacrifice anything as a concession to one another's whims....

The excuse given in all such cases, is that the "compromise" is only temporary and that one will reclaim one's integrity at some indeterminate future date. But one cannot correct a husband or wife's irrationality by giving in to it and allowing it to grow. One cannot achieve the victory of one's ideas by helping to propagate their opposite.

One cannot offer a literary masterpiece, "when one has become rich and famous," to a following one has acquired by writing trash. If one found it difficult to maintain one's loyalty to one's own convictions at the start, a succession of betrayals - which help augment the power of the evil one lacked the courage to fight - will not make it easier at a later date, but will make it virtually impossible.

There can be no compromise on moral principles. "In any compromise between food and poison, it is only death that can win. In any compromise between good and evil, it is only evil that can profit." The next time you are tempted to ask: "Doesn't life require compromise?", translate that question into it's actual meaning: Doesn't life require the surrender of that which is true and good to that which is false and evil?" The answer is that that precisely is what life forbids - if one wishes to achieve anything but a stretch of tortured years spent in progressive self-destruction." -Ayn Rand, 1962.

Food for thought, eh?   So let's get going, shall we?

From Where Do Our Rights Derive?

"The concept of individual rights is so new in human history that most men have not grasped it fully to this day. ... some men assert that rights are a gift of God - others, that rights are a gift of society. But in fact, the source of rights is man's nature. ... There is only one fundamental right (all others are it's consequences or corollaries): a man's right to his own life. Life is a process of self-sustaining and self-generated action; the right to life means the right to engage in self-sustaining and self-generated action - which means the freedom to take all the actions required by the nature of the rational being for the support, the furtherance, the fulfillment and the enjoyment of his own life. (Such is the meaning of the right to life, liberty and the pursuit of happiness.)" - Ayn Rand

The most fundamental human (individual) right there is, is your right to <u>own</u> your <u>own</u> life.

But where does it derive from?

Whether you're a theist (believe in a Supreme Being), an agnostic or an atheist, there's a derivation path for you, and the paths lead to the same conclusion – *you rightfully own your own life.*

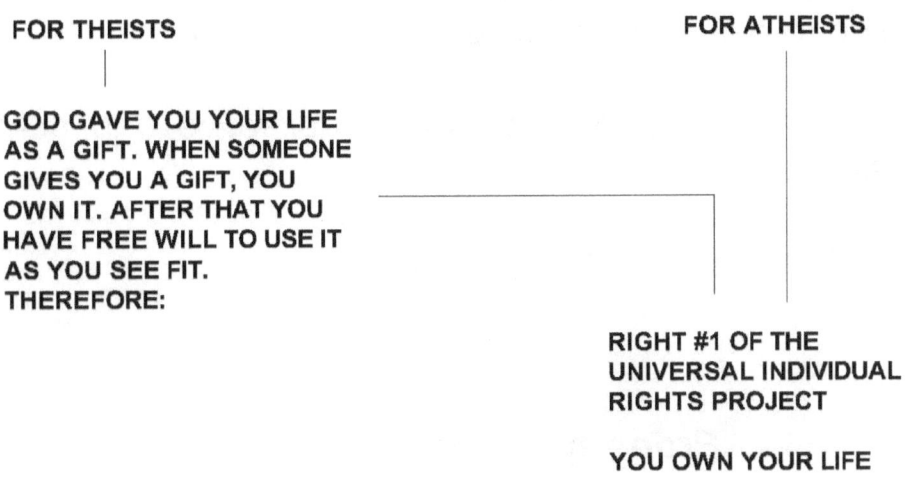

THE DERIVATION PATH OF OUR INALIENABLE INDIVIDUAL RIGHTS
AS PUT FORTH BY THE UNIVERSAL INDIVIDUAL RIGHTS PROJECT

FOR THEISTS

GOD GAVE YOU YOUR LIFE
AS A GIFT. WHEN SOMEONE
GIVES YOU A GIFT, YOU
OWN IT. AFTER THAT YOU
HAVE FREE WILL TO USE IT
AS YOU SEE FIT.
THEREFORE:

FOR ATHEISTS

RIGHT #1 OF THE
UNIVERSAL INDIVIDUAL
RIGHTS PROJECT

YOU OWN YOUR LIFE

Whichever path works for you, it boils down to one binary choice.

Either you own your life or someone else does.

If someone else does, who?

A king?

A dictator?

A collective?

Your neighbor?

If so, why should **they** own your life?

If you get through all of those things and come to the conclusion that you should rightfully own your own life, that conclusion does nothing for you unless you're willing to assert your ownership.

*If not, any ruler, dictator or collective can come along and **own** you.*

What would that make you?

A slave?

Property of another, or others?

Some variation of forced-collective property?

Can you live with that?

Some people can and some can't.

*But at the very least, they have no right to make that decision for **anyone except themselves**. After all, **they** own **their** own life, not yours.*

I've long pondered these things and have come to the conclusion that:

My own life is the highest thing of value that I can possibly own.

So it begins with that one essential principle, and the derivation leads from your assertion of your ownership of your own life, to the rest of your rights.

The Bill of Rights
of the
The Universal Individual Rights Project

(With Commentary)

Right # 1
The most fundamental human right of all.
I own my own life
Therefore I have the right to own my life

Commentary: I should rightfully be a free adult human being and therefore I demand self determination regarding how I choose to live my life, as long as I don't directly infringe the equal rights of others.

Right # 2
I have the right to own property

"Time is your total capital, and the minutes of your life are painfully few." - Robert A Heinlein

Commentary: If I should rightfully own my own life, then I should rightfully own what I spend my life to produce – the fruits of my labor – my property and my money, which is simply a commonly agreed-upon means of exchanging property. Money and property are essentially ways of storing what you spend your life to produce, therefore if you don't own your money and your private property, you don't own your life – someone else does.

"Remember that there is no such dichotomy as 'human rights' versus 'property rights.' No human rights can exist without property rights. Since material goods are produced by the mind and effort of individual men, and are needed to sustain their lives, if the producer does not own the result of his effort, he does not own his life. To deny property rights means to turn men into property owned by the state. Whoever claims the 'right' to 'redistribute' the wealth produced by others is claiming the 'right' to treat human beings as chattel." -- Ayn Rand

It should be the right of every Free Adult Individual to acquire, use, and dispose of, property in any manner that does not harm others or directly infringe their equal rights. No individual, company or government should seize or otherwise take private property, without the owner's permission or agreement of sale by the owner, except as punishment for a crime or in collection of an unpaid debt that the owner has voluntarily agreed to use the property as collateral for.

Right # 3

The right of Free Adult Individuals to keep and bear arms Shall Not Be Infringed.

Commentary: If I have the right to life, and to rightfully own my life, then I have the right to defend my life, using the most effective and modern means available.

"No free man shall ever be debarred the use of arms." - Thomas Jefferson

The right of Free Adult Individuals to defend themselves, their families, their property, and their liberty, against any and all forms of tyranny, including, but not limited to, potentially despotic governments and criminal behavior, is a "true, ancient and indubitable" human right. It should rightfully be held sacrosanct and inalienable from infringement by governments or other individuals. *This is the keystone to defending all other rights against any and all forms of tyranny.*

Right # 4

It shall be the right of every Free Adult Individual to have freedom of thought, freedom of religion, freedom of speech, freedom of the press and media, to peaceably assemble in public places, and to petition all others for redress of grievances.

In recent times, we have seen our own government here in the United States, start restricting what public places people can speak freely in, a dangerous trend. "Free speech zones" should rightfully be any and all public places.

Right # 5

The right to travel, including not only by ancient means of doing so, but by all modern means.

Commentary: Travel is a fundamental human right, and not just to travel using ancient means like walking, but as with other fundamental rights like the right to keep and bear arms and freedom of the press. It must include all of the modern means of exercising the right.

For example, it's a fundamental right to keep and bear arms, and that must include modern arms, not just black powder arms, knives, swords, sticks and rocks.

Freedom of the press and speech are fundamental rights, and they must include not just a printing press, but computers, computer printers, radio and TV.

Therefore freedom of travel is a fundamental right and must include any modern form of travel, like bicycles, cars, even planes. This does not, however, mean that anyone else must buy someone the means of exercising their rights, anymore than someone else should have to buy you a gun or computer.

Right # 6

The right of Free Adult Individuals to be secure in their persons, houses, property, own vehicles, papers, data records and effects, against unreasonable searches and seizures, shall not be violated, and no warrants shall issue, but upon probable cause, supported by oath or affirmation, and particularly describing the place to be searched, and the persons or things to be seized.

It should be noted that some states already recognize a person's own vehicle as the equivalent of their home, with regard to searches, even with regard to concealed carry of firearms.

Right # 7

No one shall be held to answer for a capital, or otherwise infamous crime, unless on a presentment or indictment of a Grand Jury, except in cases arising in the land, naval, air or space forces, or in the Militia, when in actual service in time of War or public danger; nor shall any person be subject for the same offense to be twice put in jeopardy of life or limb; nor shall be compelled in any criminal case to be a witness against himself, nor be deprived of life, liberty, or property, without the due process of laws that conform with this Bill of Rights and Constitution.

Right # 8

In all criminal prosecutions, the accused shall enjoy the right to a speedy and public trial, by an impartial jury of the State and district wherein the crime is alleged to have been committed, which district shall have been previously ascertained by law, and to be informed of the nature and cause of the accusation; to be confronted with the human witnesses against them; to have compulsory process for obtaining witnesses in their favor, and to have the Assistance of Counsel for their defense.

Right # 9

In Suits at common law, the right of trial by jury shall be preserved, and no fact tried by a jury, shall be otherwise re-examined in any Court, than according to the rules of the common law.

Right # 10

Excessive bail shall not be required, nor excessive fines imposed, nor cruel and unusual punishments inflicted.

Right # 11

If I rightfully own my own life, then I have the right to honestly marry any consenting
adult human being(s) that I choose to.

Marriage shall be the sole domain of a private contract between two or more consenting adult humans.

Commentary: If we are to be free People living in a free world, and own our lives, our relationships with other consenting adult humans must be our business and ours alone. It must be none of the business of religion, or governments, or anyone else, to dictate which consenting adult human being, or even how many, another consenting adult human being may honestly marry. (without fraud)

Right # 12

If I rightfully own my own life, then I have the right use any drug that I wish to.

Commentary: If we are to be free People living in a free world, it must be none of the business of governments, to dictate what drugs may be legal or which drugs a person may use.

Right # 13

If I rightfully own my own life then I have the right to end it, if and when I see fit, as long as I am of sound mind.

Commentary: Each adult human being should have not only the inalienable right to own their own life, but also the right to end it, if and when they see fit, providing they are of sound mind, even if for no other reason than that they are tired of living it.

Right # 14

I have the right to privacy.

Commentary: No government, company or individual shall intrude into the home or private affairs of individuals or obtain, transfer, or sell, any private personal or medical information about a person, without either that person's legally written and signed permission or the due process of a court order. No one shall take photographs or video or audio of anyone else in their home or on their property without their permission, or the permission of the property owner.

Right # 15

I own my own body

Commentary: If I rightfully own my own life, then I rightfully own my own body and I have the right to dispose of it the way I see fit, even selling my own organs if I so choose, before or after death, as long as I am of sound mind and not being coerced to do so. I also have the right to determination of what I choose to support with my own body, both internally and externally.

The author is firmly against abortion and thinks that science has proven that the life of a human being begins at conception. The proof? You can draw a continuous line from your conception, through the various stages of development, to your being born, living and eventually dying. That's your life line. I would always discourage women from having abortions, if at all possible. I would argue that it's wrong and many will suffer severe psychological consequences if they have them frivolously. Yet if we own our own bodies, people absolutely must have the final say over what they wish to have in them, and what they wish to support with them – it goes back to the most fundamental principle of self ownership in Right #1.

Right #16

The right to bear Fair Witness in public.

Titled in memory of the late Robert A Heinlein ("Stranger in a Strange Land".). Judge Andrew Napolitano of Freedom Watch was the inspiration for this right. In a free society, the People must be free to watch the government (including modern means such as video recording), but the government should not be allowed to watch the people on private property, without probable cause and a warrant.

What next then?

To back up our rights, with restraints on what governments should not be allowed to do, a Constitution is needed. This is **not** the kind of Constitution that most people are used to, by which The People give governments certain powers over them, which have historically then been expanded and abused without limits under **forced-collectivism**. This Constitution is specifically designed to be a list of things that individuals demand that governments do, shall not do, or stay out of. It must be crystal clear that this **Universal Individual Rights Project** and **Constitution Of the People of Earth**, is exactly the opposite of the socialist "one world government" model that so many of us who care about our individual rights and our liberty are so rightfully terrified of.

This whole project is intended to be a Bill of Rights that individuals all over the world can rightfully assert as their own blueprint for individual liberty. The following Constitution Of the People of Earth is intended to strengthen it, and insist that governments be restrained from having certain powers. In order for the Universal Bill of Rights to have **any** chance of succeeding, it must be tied to the following constitutional restraints on the powers of governments.

Governments should rightfully have **only** powers that do not violate the Universal Bill of Rights and that are restrained by the following Constitution.

"In questions of power, let us hear no more of the trust of men, but rather bind them down from mischief with chains of The Constitution."
– Thomas Jefferson

But as a preface I'd like to include here, most of my 2006 article, "The Litmus Test of Liberty and Morality". I think this is really important, because very few people have adequately explained to the people, the meaning and profundity of the "non-initiation of force principle", also known   as   the   "non-aggression principle".

The Litmus Test of Liberty and Morality
Is Religion Required, to Have a Moral Society?
(Revised from the original, for this publication.)

I've frequently heard and read people claiming that we need more of their religion in our schools and public life, because it's the only way to have morality taught to kids and adults, and to have a moral society. While I have nothing in particular against their religions, I disagree, in fact many of the most immoral people I've ever met also claimed to be "religious".

(This doesn't mean that religion is, in and of itself, "bad", it just means that it doesn't have an exclusive claim, or franchise on morality.)

And can't an atheist or agnostic also be moral? Religion certainly can teach morality, but it doesn't have an exclusive claim on doing so.

Morality only requires good philosophy, and in fact it can be totally independent of religion. As Ayn Rand explained in "Philosophy: Who Needs It" (Her Address To The Graduating Class Of The United States Military Academy at West Point, New York - March 6, 1974) , philosophy is comprised of several factors including ethics and aesthetics. Good philosophy is what you really need to be moral, whether it comes with religion or without it.

And what of liberty? Do we really have liberty in a forced-collectivist society, where slavery and involuntary servitude are legalized monopolies of government?

Is that free or moral?

We have literally millions of laws here in the United States, most of which impose slavery and involuntary servitude on our people in some form or another, and the rest of the world is the same, if not worse.

We have so many laws that even the politicians who passed them don't know what they all say or mean.

The Congress meets every year and continues to pass an ever-increasing number of them, without sunsets (expiration dates) and without end.

"It will be of little avail to people that the laws are made by men of their own choice, if the laws be so voluminous that they cannot be understood; or if they be repealed or revised before they are promulgated , or undergo such incessant changes that no man knows what it will be tomorrow... Frequent changes give an unreasonable advantage to the sagacious, enterprising, and moneyed few, over the industrious and uninformed masses of the people." – James Madison

Does that sound familiar?

I've always been told by statists (State worshipers, the way I see it.), that in effect, I, a mere mortal and subject of the rule of government, am so far beneath the ivory tower that I'm too stupid, incompetent or dishonest to be able to tell right from wrong on my own. After all, who am I?

(Yet, who were the founders of the United States, if not mere common mortals, who were told the same thing about their relationship to their king?)

No, the lawyers, politicians and especially the Supreme Court, are the only ones who are qualified to "hand down" from high, their opinions to me, on what those millions of laws really mean, and I must accept their "rulings" over me.

But I don't think it really needs to be that complicated and I think I have a great litmus test, elegant in its simplicity, for sorting things out for myself. I don't need the ivory "tower of Babel" and all of its lawyers and politicians to dictate to me what's moral and define my freedom for me.

So What's the litmus test?

What I've thought of as "true Libertarians", and Objectivists **know** what it is. It's called the Non-INITIATION of Force principle (also known as the NAP – Non-Aggression Principle) and it's common to both of those philosophies, or at least to those who are true to Libertarianism.

"Who is a libertarian?

A libertarian is a person who believes that no one has the right, under any circumstances, to initiate force against another human being, or to advocate or delegate its initiation. Those who act consistently with this principle are libertarians, whether they realize it or not. Those who fail to act consistently with it are not libertarians, regardless of what they may claim." - L. Neil Smith

"The basic political principle of the Objectivist ethics is: no man may initiate the use of physical force against others." - Ayn Rand

It's the simple principle that it's morally wrong to **initiate force** or to **delegate its initiation**. I don't need the politicians and their millions of laws. I don't need the courts to "interpret" for my poor lowly "unwashed" peon mind. All I need is that one defining Litmus Test of Liberty and Morality.

Yet as simple as it is, probably only a few percent of the American public could agree to that principle, especially when they understood its implications. How sad that is. That's exactly why we're in the mess we're in today.

"Peace, commerce, and honest friendship with all nations - entangling alliances with none." -Thomas Jefferson.

The non-initiation of force principle was understood at a very basic level by Jefferson, it underlies much of our Constitution and Bill of Rights, and the reason that so much within those documents is being routinely ignored now, is that the politicians have abandoned that principle and have chosen to turn this country from the constitutional republic that it began as, into a pure poll-driven populist mob rule democracy.

It's been said that a democracy is three wolves and a sheep, voting on what's for dinner. This is why our founders very carefully avoided a democracy and established a <u>Constitutional Republic</u> instead.

"Our legislators are not sufficiently apprised of the rightful limits of their powers; that their true office is to declare and enforce only our natural rights and duties, and to take none of them from us. No man has a natural right to commit aggression on the equal rights of another; and this is all from which the laws ought to restrain him. Every man is under the natural duty of contributing to the necessities of the society; and this is all the laws should enforce on him. And, no man having a natural right to be the judge between himself and another, it is his natural duty to submit to the umpirage of an impartial third. When the laws have declared and enforced all this, they have fulfilled their functions, and the idea is quite unfounded that on entering into society we give up any natural right. - Thomas Jefferson

The following are modern truisms that were previously attributed as quotes, but have since been disconnected with the people they were allegedly quoted from. Nevertheless, they serve to illustrate the points I'm getting at here:

A democracy is nothing more than mob rule, where fifty one percent of the people may take away the rights of the other forty nine.

A democracy cannot exist as a permanent form of government. It can only exist until the voters discover that they can vote themselves gifts from the public treasury. From that moment on, the majority always votes for the candidates promising them the most benefits from the public treasury, with the result that a democracy always collapses over loose fiscal policy, always followed by a dictatorship.

Sound familiar?

"The merit of our Constitution was, not that it promotes democracy, but checks it." - Horatio Seymour

And one of the most recent and profound expressions of these sentiments:

"We have allowed our constitutional republic to deteriorate into a virtually unchecked direct democracy. Today's political process is nothing more than a street fight between various groups seeking to vote themselves other people's money. Individual voters tend to support the candidate that promises them the most federal loot in whatever form, rather than the candidate who will uphold the rule of law." - Rep. Ron Paul

I think that the Progressive Socialist movement, starting back around the time of President Theodore Roosevelt, has had the agenda of slowly "transforming" America from a Constitutional Republic into a pure democracy, for the very reasons above.

So we now have millions of laws, in what amounts to a legal tower of Babel, and our Constitution and Bill of Rights are being routinely ignored for what amounts to pure populist poll driven mob rule democracy.

This country, indeed the entire world at this point, is in very deep trouble, and I assert to you that there's only one way out, short of the eventual disintegration of this country and possibly a violent forced-collectivist revolutionary period, where we could wind up with no more United States.

There is an urgent need to get back to recognizing, and living by, the real principles of liberty that started this country and once made it great.

It is with that purpose that this Project was written, so that we may not only do that, but modernize it and offer it to the whole world, not just the United States.

"In questions of power, let us hear no more of the trust of men, but rather bind them down from mischief with chains of The Constitution." - Thomas Jefferson

Please recognize that the Non-INITIATION of Force principle is the litmus test of liberty and morality and that we don't need the corrupt politicians or the courts to dictate those things to us, all we need is that simple test that we can all carry around in our minds.

The Kicker – The Conundrum

The problem is that, while a lot of people would agree that it's basically morally wrong to initiate force against others or delegate its initiation (via government) , when they understand the implications (like a nation and government involving voluntary relationships and voluntary collectivism, instead of forced-collectivism, run with voluntary contributions instead of taxes - which amount to involuntary servitude, initiation of force and slavery), they really can't get on board with it.

You see, as Ron Paul pointed out, most people **like** having their hands in everyone else's pockets, even if others have their hands in theirs, and they **like** the **power and control** of forming a mob and dictating how they think everyone else should live.

"What is ominous is the ease with which some people go from saying that they don't like something to saying that the government should forbid it. When you go down that road, don't expect freedom to survive very long." -- Thomas Sowell (Another hero of mine.)

But as **long** as most people think that initiating force is OK, we **will** have the loss of freedom, to that extent, and government will **always** remain out of the control of the people, with the power to do virtually **anything** they **please** to us.

This one crucial principle stands as the dividing line between liberty and slavery. Without it, no government anywhere can possibly be limited by the freedom or will of the people.

"...a wise and frugal government, which shall restrain men from injuring one another, which shall leave them otherwise free to regulate their own pursuits of industry and improvement, and shall not take from the mouth of labor the bread it has earned. This is the sum of good government." - Thomas Jefferson (1801)

The Major Implications of The Kicker

It has been said that *"the power to tax is the power to destroy"*. This is because **the power to tax is the power to initiate force against "The People"**. Once that genie is unleashed, government is, by its very nature and structure of "the system" illimitable. We see vast examples of this in the world today. Here in the United States, we have a Constitution which was a work of genius in its day - it still is! Yet it's routinely ignored and considered irrelevant by many, if not most of our politicians – in effect rulers, who because of the power to tax, can safely ignore it, because **they have nearly unlimited power to initiate force against us!**

I run into people all the time, who say to me that "the system is good, it just has some problems and needs to be fixed. We just have to vote for the right people and work hard to get them elected.".

Well I'm afraid that I have bad news for these people. Voters have been working, based on that premise for how long now? How's that effort working out for you?

There's an old saying that; "Insanity is doing the same thing over and over again and expecting different results."

The system can't be fixed by just voting the "right" people into office, because the system is forced-collectivist.

The system is the problem.

That's the nature of the beast!

"In this present crisis, government is not the solution to our problem; government is the problem. From time to time we've been tempted to believe that society has become too complex to be managed by self-rule, that government by an elite group is superior to government for, by, and of the people. Well, if no one among us is capable of governing himself, then who among us has the capacity to govern someone else?" - President Ronald Reagan, First Inaugural Address

And I assert to you that the non-initiation of force principle is the dividing line between controllable workable government and the out-of-control mess and mindless **beast** that we have now.

Please think about this for awhile. Take as long as you need. It's true but it takes some time and thought to get past the cognitive dissonance (The feeling that it "does not compute!") that's been conditioned into all of us by our forced-collectivist society since birth!

People have inalienable rights, not governments. Governments have **only** those powers given to them by "The People". **At the point where The People give government the power to initiate force, that is the very point that government begins the moral decline (or rise to illimitable power) towards eventually becoming an out-of-control monster or Beast.**

So I submit to you that there's only one way to **ever** get that genie back in the box again - to get the government back under the control of The People - and that way is to demand **relentlessly** that no government, anywhere on earth, can ever again have the power given to it by "The People", to **initiate force.**

The following is a secret, to most people:

If "We The People" heed this advice, we will have inalienable individual rights and freedom.

If we do not, you will eventually see "global governance" and the most utter oppression, poverty, slavery, misery and death that the world has ever known, because it won't just be limited to nations that can be isolated anymore (like North Korea, Cuba...) it will be global!

**Please - Mark my words on this!
The non-initiation of force principle, backed by a
rational philosophy – Objectivism, is
the <u>only</u> way to <u>ever</u> achieve this!**

The quickest thing that I've seen happen to people who advocate any variation of the theme that government should not be allowed to initiate force, is that someone pops up immediately and accuses them of being an "anarchist". I witnessed this happening during a discussion panel where **Nick Gillespie** of **Reason Magazine** was appearing, and he quickly exclaimed that he wasn't an anarchist. But of course, because so many TV shows consist of sound bites, he wasn't given time to explain. So let's explain here.

Why is not allowing government to initiate force, which would have to include removing their power to tax, <u>not</u> anarchy?

Over the past twenty years, as my thinking slowly evolved on these issues, from being a '60's liberal to being an Objectivist now, I engaged in many online discussions with actual anarchists and libertarians.

Many of them hadn't worked out this issue in their own minds, and instead called themselves by labels like "minarchist" (advocate of small government) or anarcho-capitalist (advocate of no government - just a world with totally free markets). They absolutely couldn't see the point that I eventually put on my chart at the beginning of this book. That's the totally sweet spot between the various degrees of forced-collectivism (loss of liberty) and anarchy (so much liberty that people abused it, and it ends up wrapping back around to forced-collectivism).

That sweet spot is the point where government is not allowed to initiate force (which includes taxation.), and must run solely on voluntary contributions, thus starving it of the power to do anything it pleases and to become that out-of-control monster Beast that we've seen whenever such powers <u>inevitably</u> increase to the point of extreme abuse.

The following is a short piece that I put together as a sort of macro, to help quickly and concisely explain it:

"The power to tax is the power to destroy" your life, your prosperity and your liberty. There's only one way to **ever** limit government.

How?

Voluntary Government

<u>Only</u> the amount of government that the people would willingly support, and that wasn't allowed to initiate force. Before you scoff at the idea and start saying that no one would support it, think about it some.

Everything the government currently does, which people wouldn't voluntarily support it doing, all the waste and pork would be gone, leaving perhaps 5-10% of the budget that government has now, which could **only** be used for the essentials that people **<u>would</u>** willingly support. Therefore they'd likely have more funding for the things the people **<u>really</u>** wanted, without all the waste and oppression of human rights that the government does now.

How would it be done?

The forced-collectivists think that Uncle Sam would have to stand on a corner holding a hat out for donations, but that's absurd hyperbole.

It could be done similarly to how government is supported now, only voluntarily. People could make a flat suggested donation for their income level, at work, through payroll deductions, **or** they could make a suggested donation at the store when they buy things, <u>or</u> they might even go on their computers and itemize certain percentages or amounts of their payroll donations for certain things, like defense, police, fire, courts, or roads - the **essential** things that they really wanted government doing for them.

They would be free, instead of being enslaved to support every frivolous whim that some enormously powerful politician (who had been allowed to initiate force and borrow, tax and spend without limits) might dream up, like everyone is **forced** to do now.

And the marxist motto "From each according to his abilities, to each according to his needs." would be eliminated, as they would no longer be **forced into slavery to pay for every imagined "need" and crony support, that anyone else could dream up.**

The voluntary government plan above would be **perfect** because people would only get the amount of government they'd voluntarily support, thereby eliminating all pork and whims.

Think about this following statement. <u>If</u> we have a "government of the People, by the People, and for the People", then:

Any amount of government that the People won't <u>willingly</u> (voluntarily) support, doesn't deserve to exist.

Think about that, the elegance of it!

I call this "the sweet spot of liberty".

If we phased over to **a government run solely on voluntary contributions, that wasn't allowed to initiate force**, instead of what we have now, we could gain control again, over the out-of-control monster that government has become, **before it destroys us all. And we're getting dangerously close to that point and time, right now!**

"Listen, what's the most horrible experience you can imagine? To me – it's being left, unarmed, in a sealed cell with a drooling beast of prey or a maniac who's had some disease that's eaten his brain out. You'd have nothing then but your voice – your voice and your thought. You'd scream to that creature why it should not touch you, you'd have the most eloquent words, the unanswerable words, you'd become the vessel of the absolute truth. And you'd see living eyes watching you and you'd know that the thing can't hear you, that it can't be reached, not reached, not in any way, yet it's breathing and moving there before you with a purpose of its own. That's horror. Well, that's what's hanging over the world, prowling somewhere through mankind, that same thing, something closed, mindless, utterly wanton, but something with an aim and a cunning of its own." – Steven Mallory, The Fountainhead, by Ayn Rand

So with that being said, and hopefully fully understood, it's time to move on to the proposed new Constitution. I'm calling this the "proposed new Constitution", not only because no one except myself has adopted it yet, but because it, as well as the Universal Individual Rights Project, was developed solely by me so far, solely by one single individual.

I'm not arrogant to think that it's absolutely perfect, that it couldn't use a little fine-tuning. It was done without the help of lawyers or politicians. A few people online, who heard of me developing it, made a few suggestions, which I've fine-tuned a couple of things with, and you can tell that a few of the rights and articles have been derived from the United States Constitution, but most of it is my own creation.

So if this book finds anyone at all interested in helping me carry the ball forward now, my plans are to start up a World Headquarters for this Project and fine tune what needs fine-tuning, translate it into other languages, and present it to people across the world.

Like I've already made very clear, this is not meant to be a blueprint for a world government, in fact just the opposite. It's meant to be a blueprint for individuals, and perhaps governments around the world, to adopt for themselves. Any individual can adopt it and become an advocate for it, at any time, because free will, not forced-collectivism, is involved.

Because it's based on what I passionately believe are the most essential and pure principles of liberty that have ever existed, <u>any government can also adopt it and practice it, at any time, without even holding a vote of its own population</u>.

Why?

Because they would be agreeing to limit their government to the most essential principles of liberty, which include ending the initiation of force against their own people, including taxation, so they would be setting their people free instead of enslaving them!

Voting is only essential and extremely important to people when they form a mob and vote on the various ways they want to initiate force against others!

Someone I met online years ago, said to me that if the non-initiation of force principle was applied to government, voting would cease to be anywhere near as important as it is to us now.

Why?

Because, as Ron Paul pointed out, voting is now, and has always been used as a tool to initiate force against others, to use the force of government to coerce people into giving up percentages of their lives to support the "needs", perceived needs, whims and even follies (pork, earmarks, etc....) and cronies of other people and special interest groups.

For example, who would support farm subsidies where farmers were paid **not** to grow things, **knowing that it would only raise the cost of those things at the supermarkets? No one.**

Who would give money to nations that hate us, and would use the money against us, and to give to the friends of the dictators in power?

No one.

Who would give money to support a "bridge to nowhere", for "art" work that was horrible and offensive, or to study shrimps running on tread mills? **No one.**

In a forced-collectivist system, government can take as much of your money as it pleases (involuntary servitude/slavery) and do anything it pleases with it.

For stunning examples, we recommend "Wastebook", by Senator Tom Coburn, M.D., last seen at:

http://www.coburn.senate.gov/public/index.cfm/pre ssreleases?ContentRecord_id=f9478504-be7e-4b8f-9ef8-baa0895a9579

If government was no longer **allowed** to initiate force, all of that would be gone, so voting would be **far** less important. We'd have **only** the amount of government, doing **only** the **legitimate** things (not allowed to initiate force) that people would **voluntarily** support them doing, and not a bit more.

Voting might be about the issue of what color to paint the court house, or how the funds that people contributed to the general fund, and they became surplus, would now be used. But without the initiation of force and the power to tax, no government would have money for wild frivolous whims or wars.

Any wars could only be defensive, and would only defend the nation that was having force initiated against it by another nation that had not yet accepted these principles of freedom and non-Aggression.

So with that in mind, it's time to move on to the new proposed Constitution.

The Constitution of the People of Earth
C.O.P.E.
The Chains of the Constitution

Article 1

Non-Aggression

No government or individual shall initiate physical force, or advocate, delegate or tolerate its initiation.

Commentary:

Let me preface this commentary by saying that it's very important to examine the word "initiate" in this principle. It does not mean that defensive or retaliatory force should not, or cannot be used. In fact:

"The necessary consequence of man's right to life is his right to self-defense. In a civilized society, force may be used only in retaliation & only against those who initiate its use. All the reasons which make the initiation of physical force an evil, make the retaliatory use of physical force a moral imperative. If some 'pacifist' society renounced the retaliatory use of force, it would be left helplessly at the mercy of the 1st thug who decided to be immoral. Such a society would achieve the opposite of its intention: instead of abolishing evil, it would encourage & reward it." - Ayn Rand "The Nature of Government" (1961)

But the non-aggression principle, also known as the non-initiation of force principle, is one of the most fundamental and important principles of liberty.

In fact I've called it

"The Litmus Test of Liberty".

Nowadays, people talk about how to limit the size of government, yet without this very simple principle it is illimitable, and here's why:

"The Constitution is either a superior, paramount law, unchangeable by ordinary means, or it is on a level with ordinary legislative acts and, like other acts, is alterable when the legislature shall please to alter it. If the former part of the alternative be true, then a legislative act contrary to the Constitution is not law; if the latter part be true, then written constitutions are absurd attempts, on the part of the people, to limit a power in its own nature illimitable." Thus, the Constitution is either The Supreme Law of the Land, superceding all other laws, or the Constitution is a worthless piece of paper. If the latter, government can do as it pleases. If the former, tyrants have seized sovereignty illegally, it is the duty of the people to put them in their proper place in history. - Chief Justice of the Supreme Court, John Marshall - 1803

Yet despite Constitutions, governments have managed to grow without limits. Why? Because they are allowed to initiate force against their own people. One of the wisest things I've ever seen written, is that governments should not be allowed to do anything that, if you or I did them, would be considered criminal. For example, holding someone at gunpoint and taking their money.

"Two men have no more natural right to exercise any kind of authority over one, than one has to exercise the same authority over two. A man's natural rights are his own, against the whole world; and any infringement of them is equally a crime; whether committed by one man, or by millions; whether committed by one man, calling himself a robber, (or by any other name indicating his true character), or by millions calling themselves a government." - Lysander Spooner

"Since the protection of individual rights is the only proper purpose of a government, it is the only proper subject of legislation: all laws must be based on individual rights and aimed at their protection." – Ayn Rand

"The basic political principle of the Objectivist ethics is: no man may initiate the use of physical force against others." - Ayn Rand

Once governments are allowed the power to initiate force against individuals or other nations, there is no way of limiting their powers. Not how much they spend, not how much they consume from the People, not how much war they make, not how much they infringe human liberty. Not any of it.

Note: Fraud for material gain is also included in this principle, as it is theft by deception.

Article 2

There shall be no slavery or involuntary servitude, including a military draft.

Military conscription is involuntary servitude and slavery. A nation that can't be defended with volunteers, isn't worth defending. Military conscription is contrary to human rights and self-ownership.

Article 3

The right of a free adult **citizen** to vote and otherwise participate in governmental processes shall not be infringed in any manner or for any reason. No issue allowing the initiation of force shall be on any ballot.

Article 4

No government shall make or keep any laws either establishing or promoting a state religion, or a particular religion, or infringing the practice of any religion, as long as the religion is not initiating force against others.

Article 5

No government shall make or enforce any law which shall abridge the privileges or immunities of its citizens; nor shall any government deprive any person of life, liberty, or property, without due process of law; nor deny to any person within its jurisdiction the equal protection of laws that conform with this Bill of Rights and Constitution.

Article 6

No government, company or individual shall intrude into the home or private affairs of individuals or obtain, transfer, or sell, any private personal or medical information about a person, without either that person's legally written and signed permission or a court order.

Article 7

It has long been the practice of governments and central banks like our Federal Reserve, to devalue money by not basing it on anything of value and constantly expanding it's supply. Since the formation of the Federal Reserve in 1913, the dollar has lost about 95% of its value! This robs people of the value of their currency, their life savings, investors of their investments, and defrauds and steals from lenders. It amounts to theft. Currency – money must have real value.

Therefore:

There shall be no central bank.

All legal currency must be backed by precious metals, or equivalent value of other materials of value. There shall be no fiat money.

Article 8

Unconstitutional Laws Need Not Be Obeyed By Good People.

If a law violates inalienable individual rights No one has a moral obligation to obey it.

Throughout history, governments and individuals have violated human (individual) rights. When governments have done so, it has often been accompanied by passage of laws to enforce such violations, under the authority people allow governments. Examples are the slavery laws in the early U.S. and laws violating the human rights of Jews and others during the period of Nazi Germany. During these, and other such times, there were brave people who realized the immorality of such laws and because the laws violated human rights, they felt no obligation to obey them.

Therefore:

No one has any moral obligation to obey any law that violates human rights.

Any and all laws that violate human rights should be immediately repealed.

Article 9

**No law shall be made or kept,
abridging freedom of production or trade.**

(Paraphrased from "Atlas Shrugged" by Ayn Rand)

Article 10

It has been the practice of governments to borrow their people into bankruptcy and then tax and/or print fiat money to compensate for it, placing burdens on The People as well as future generations. Therefore:

All governments shall maintain balanced budgets on a yearly basis.

Article 11

No government shall have deficit spending.

Article 12

No government shall be in debt.

No government shall loan money to, insure, or buy stocks or bonds from, any private person, any private or partly private entity, or any other government.

No government shall guarantee payment of any such financial instruments. No government shall pay or subsidize interest, premiums, principal, dividends or any other aspect of any such financial instrument.

Article 13

No troops shall ever be housed or stationed on private property without the permission of the owner(s). If they do so, the community may consider them rogues.

Article 14

No free person's property shall be taken or bought, without the owner's permission. There shall be no eminent domain laws.

Article 15

If someone is imprisoned and later set free, all their human rights shall be restored again, including but not limited to the right to keep and bear arms.

If someone is still considered a danger to themselves or others, they should remain locked up. It's wrong to infringe the human rights of free people.

Article 16

Marriage shall be the sole domain of a private contract between two or more consenting adult humans. No government shall dictate any terms outside of these or refuse to recognize such contractual marriage.

Think about this one. Why should it be the business of government or religion, to dictate over private voluntary (consensual) agreements between two or more consenting adults?

Article 17

Government In The Sunshine

All government proceedings, except those involving the highest levels of secrecy for national security, shall be open to the public.

Article 18

Sunset of Laws

All laws, with the exception of high crimes, shall expire automatically after a period of five years from the date they were passed, unless reconsidered and renewed. All such laws that were passed more than five years before the adoption of this Constitution will be void, upon its passage.

Article 19

All laws shall consist of a single topic.

**All previous laws must be converted
to single topics or repealed.**

How many times have we seen laws that were thousands of pages, loaded with pork, earmarks and special interest gifts and baggage. To avoid this, laws should stick to the point and consist of one topic per law.

Article 20

All new laws shall be tested and shall pass a test for constitutionality, by the judiciary, <u>before</u> being signed into law.

This article was inspired by Judge Andrew Napolitano of Freedom Watch.

Article 21

Unions shall not be allowed in any government or governmental agency.

This article was inspired by FDR, of all people, who was one of the most socialist Presidents.

"A few timid people, who fear progress, will try to give you new and strange names for what we are doing. Sometimes they will call it "Fascism," sometimes "Communism," sometimes "Regimentation," sometimes "Socialism."" - FDR

"I don't regard Communism as an evil. Some of my best friends are Communists. I think Russia is a fine, great country and I admire Stalin." -- Franklin D. Roosevelt, to Senator Martin Dies, the White House, 1939

Yes, even FDR, who many now consider to have been a Progressive socialist, warned against unions being allowed into government. We now face the collapse of federal, local, state and some global economies because of pension deals that were negotiated between governments and government employee unions. These were deals in which the union employees were never required to put as much of their own funds into pensions, and were often allowed to retire much earlier than non-governmental employees - in effect given much for actually earning far less.

It actually sparked a practice called "double dipping", in which the employees "retire" early, then take other jobs – sometimes even in governments, to make double incomes.

This was often tied in with political support for the politicians, most of whom are long gone, who promised them these gifts from the public treasury in return for their votes.

"All Government employees should realize that the process of collective bargaining, as usually understood, cannot be transplanted into the public service. It has its distinct and insurmountable limitations when applied to public personnel management. The very nature and purposes of Government make it impossible for administrative officials to represent fully or to bind the employer in mutual discussions with Government employee organizations. The employer is the whole people, who speak by means of laws enacted by their representatives in Congress. Accordingly, administrative officials and employees alike are governed and guided, and in many instances restricted, by laws which establish policies, procedures, or rules in personnel matters.

...

"Particularly, I want to emphasize my conviction that militant tactics have no place in the functions of any organization of Government employees. Upon employees in the Federal service rests the obligation to serve the whole people, whose interests and welfare require orderliness and continuity in the conduct of Government activities. This obligation is paramount. Since their own services have to do with the functioning of the Government, a strike of public employees manifests nothing less than an intent on their part to prevent or obstruct the operations of Government until their demands are satisfied. Such action, looking toward the paralysis of Government by those who have sworn to support it, is unthinkable and intolerable. It is, therefore, with a feeling of gratification that I have noted in the constitution of the National Federation of Federal Employees the provision that "under no circumstances shall this Federation engage in or support strikes against the United States Government." - "FDR" - President Franklin Delano Roosevelt

Article 22

Except in the case of defense and response to an actual incoming nuclear attack, war must be declared, against a specific enemy and with specifically defined goals.

"I've often argued that we don't have a two party system in this country any longer. We have one party - the Big Government Party. It has a Democratic wing that believes in taxes and individual welfare and assaulting commercial liberties and war. It has a Republican wing that believes in defecits and corporate welfare and assaulting civil liberties and war. Neither wing believes in personal freedom, they both love telling us how to live, they both love the Federal Reserve and they both love staying in power." - Judge Andrew Napolitano, on his show Freedom Watch

One of the greatest fears that the founders of the United States had, was of a standing army. In modern times, we see a standing army as inevitable, but the question becomes: How can we avoid being in a constant state of war?

We've seen exactly that in the decades since World War II, the last declared war that the United States fought in. The reason lies greatly in the fact that governments are allowed to initiate force, and also greatly in the fact that formal declarations of war have not been required by our Congress.

Strict adherence to this article, combined with the non-initiation of force principle, should prevent that.

Article 23

NOTA Voting – None Of The Above.

In all elections, "NOTA – None Of The Above" shall be on the ballot as a last resort option for each candidate position being voted on. If a majority of voters vote for "NOTA – None Of The Above", the election for that position shall be re-held in 90 days, and all of the candidates who ran the first time shall be ineligible in follow-up votes for that office.

Conclusions

People around the world need to decide whether they want a society where governments and their cronies control all the wealth and rule over The People as slaves, or whether they could be happier in a world where everyone was free and prosperous.

I think that the more honest and sincere of governments will eventually be willing to evolve to a new level, stop imposing infringements on rightful liberties of The People, and adopt the blueprint put forth here.

Others may choose to oppress their people for awhile longer, in various degrees of poverty, misery, slavery and death. I can only hope that their people will learn of other options like this, and will retire them peacefully from power, so that the people may be free at last.

"You can't hold a man down without staying down with him." - Booker T. Washington.

"Tax the rich, feed the poor
Till there are no rich no more"
- 10 Years After

All the wealth in the United States, or in the rest of the world, could be taken away from the people who spent their lives to produce it, and redistributed, and almost everyone would then be poor. (Except for those in power who perpetrated the evil deed, and their friends - you can bet on that.)

Instead of bringing America down, as many of the more extreme forced-collectivists would like to do, I think that the answer lies in bringing everyone in the world up.

Or as a popular modern American patriot recently illustrated; It's not a matter of dividing up a finite pie into tiny enough portions so that everyone can have a grain of it, its a matter of teaching everyone how to make their own pie.

That's a take-off of:

*"Give a man a fish and you feed him for a day.
Teach a man to fish and you feed him for a lifetime."*

I think that it absolutely starts with a worldwide goal of 100% literacy, and that it can then eventually become fully realized by using the blueprint of the principles of this Project.

"A government big enough to give you everything you want is a government big enough to take from you everything you have." - President Gerald Ford

As you've seen with recent events in Egypt and other middle eastern countries, we now face an *absolutely crucial* time in the history of the world.

Government has grown so large that it threatens to consume everything we have, and everything that future generations will ever earn in the future.

Spread the word:

*IF the world's population are **not** educated to appreciate the essential principles of liberty, and **soon,** it means potentially a **totalitarian global dictatorship** for future generations, with tens of millions, perhaps billions of people murdered by government.*

Think about it.

If you don't want to be ruled by dictators...

"A Bill Of Rights is what the people are entitled to <u>against</u> every government on earth, general or particular, and what no just government should refuse, or rest on inference." -Thomas Jefferson

It is for this reason that I think it is crucial to get the word out about this project right away, and start promoting it around the world.

I think that if the founders of the United States could go forward in some kind of time machine and see what the world and the nation they founded have become, they would think long and hard and would eventually adopt this Blueprint in its entirety. I tried to write this, with that in mind.

I was "born in the U.S.A." and have lived here all of my life. I think that the good things about us, including our heritage of individual rights, make us unique in history, and most people around the world know it.

http://www.canadafreepress.com/

"*Because without America* there is no Free World"

This is why, instead of like in some of the Communist "slave pens" of the past, and sadly the present, instead of building walls and fences to keep people **in**, at times we've built walls and fences to keep people out.

But my dream and vision is that we can promote *universal literacy* **and** the *principles in this book*, and that so many people and nations will read, appreciate and adopt them that we may someday see a world without, not only walls and fences, but without borders even being necessary any longer, and without the proposed globalist one-world government tyranny, because individual rights and liberty will rule, and bring all the people of our world, for the first time in human history, peace, prosperity and above all, the ultimate in freedom.

As of this writing, the United States is facing another even more dismal Presidential election season. But unlike previous years, there don't even appear to be any more "lesser of evils" choices to vote for – they all seem evil now. As explained in this book, it's not simply a matter of "finding the right people to vote for and voting for the right people" - it's the system. What we're witnessing is the eventual destination of any and all forced-collectivist systems. The system is gradually disintegrating and will eventually collapse into chaos.

So now, we've come to a time when the only choice is between good and evil. Which will you choose?

Yours in the struggle for Liberty, Peace and Prosperity,

Kira Saoirse
The Universal Individual Rights Project
First Edition of the Book
Copyright July 4th, 2016
All Rights Reserved

The Declaration of Independence (Excerpt)

"IN CONGRESS, July 4, 1776.

The unanimous Declaration of the thirteen united States of America,

When in the Course of human events, it becomes necessary for one people to dissolve the political bands which have connected them with another, and to assume among the powers of the earth, the separate and equal station to which the Laws of Nature and of Nature's God entitle them, a decent respect to the opinions of mankind requires that they should declare the causes which impel them to the separation.

We hold these truths to be self-evident, that all men are created equal, that they are endowed by their Creator with certain unalienable Rights, that among these are Life, Liberty and the pursuit of Happiness.--That to secure these rights, Governments are instituted among Men, deriving their just powers from the consent of the governed, --That whenever any Form of Government becomes destructive of these ends, it is the Right of the People to alter or to abolish it, and to institute new Government, laying its foundation on such principles and organizing its powers in such form, as to them shall seem most likely to effect their Safety and Happiness. Prudence, indeed, will dictate that Governments long established should not be changed for light and transient causes; and accordingly all experience hath shewn, that mankind are more disposed to suffer, while evils are sufferable, than to right themselves by abolishing the forms to which they are accustomed. But when a long train of abuses and usurpations, pursuing invariably the same Object evinces a design to reduce them under absolute Despotism, it is their right, it is their duty, to throw off such Government, and to provide new Guards for their future security."

"Tell them in England, if they ask
What brought us to these wars,
To this plateau beneath the night's
Grave manifold of stars

It was not fraud or foolishness,
Glory, revenge, or pay:
We came because our open eyes
Could see no other way.

There was no other way to keep
Man's flickering truth alight:
These stars will witness that our course
Burned briefer, not less bright.

Beyond the wasted olive-groves,
The furthest lift of land,
There calls a country that was ours
And here shall be regained...."

"The Volunteer"
Cecil Day Lewis

Food For Thought - Awareness Snippets

Have you often wondered why American Presidential Elections are huge, expensive, lavish extravaganzas, reminiscent of the Movie "Hunger Games"? We, here at The Universal Individual Rights Project think that a large part of it is because you're giving your consent to be ruled, and they want validation of that, by as many voters as possible.:

"Then I saw what was wrong with the world, I saw what destroyed men and nations, and where the battle for life had to be fought. I saw that the enemy was an inverted morality—and that my sanction was its only power. I saw that evil was impotent—that evil was the irrational, the blind, the anti-real—and that the only weapon of its triumph was the willingness of the good to serve it. Just as the parasites around me were proclaiming their helpless dependence on my mind and were expecting me voluntarily to accept a slavery they had no power to enforce, just as they were counting on my self-immolation to provide them with the means of their plan—so throughout the world and throughout men's history, in every version and form, from the extortions of loafing relatives to the atrocities of collectivized countries, it is the good, the able, the men of reason, who act as their own destroyers, who transfuse to evil the blood of their virtue and let evil transmit to them the poison of destruction, thus gaining for evil the power of survival, and for their own values—the impotence of death. I saw that there comes a point, in the defeat of any man of virtue, when his own consent is needed for evil to win— and that no manner of injury done to him by others can succeed if he chooses to withhold his consent.

I saw that I could put an end to your outrages by pronouncing a single word in my mind. I pronounced it. The word was "No."" - John Galt, from "Atlas Shrugged", by Ayn Rand.

This doesn't mean that you shouldn't vote, because the system remains the same forced-collectivist one, no matter who you vote for. If you want to live free, the system must be changed. Forced-collectivism must be ended.

"Contemplate the mangled bodies of your countrymen, and then say, 'What should be the reward of such sacrifices?' Bid us and our posterity bow the knee, supplicate the friendship, and plough, and sow, and reap, to glut the avarice of the men who have let loose on us the dogs of war to riot in our blood and hunt us from the face of the earth? If ye love wealth better than liberty, the tranquility of servitude than the animating contest of freedom, go from us in peace. We ask not your counsel nor your arms. Crouch down and lick the hands which feed you. May your chains sit lightly upon you, and may posterity forget that ye were our countrymen!" -- Samuel Adams

"Left and right are just wings of the same forced-collectivist bird, that flies at tax slave expense." - Kira Saoirse

I once heard that "Success is the progressive realization of positive worthwhile goals". It was the best definition of the word that I have ever found. If it's not positive and worthwhile, it cannot be "success". - Kira Saoirse

"Americans have been awash in a tsunami of anti-rights philosophy for more than 100 years, and the tsunami has taken its toll. Americans no longer have the conviction that we have rights and thus no longer have the conviction that the government must protect our rights. . . . Fortunately, we have a solution to this problem: Objectivism, the philosophy that supports the principle of rights and anchors it in perceptual reality. If a small minority of intelligent, active-minded Americans come to understand and advocate this philosophy, we can, over time, turn the tide and reestablish a rights-respecting republic with a foreign policy of rational self-defense. Please join the effort." —Craig Biddle

"Having government do things for you is like giving yourself a blood transfusion from your right arm to your left, and losing half of it on the way." - Jimmy Carter

The right of the people to keep and bear arms shall not be infringed, and this without any qualification as to their condition or degree, as is the case in the British government. -- This may be considered as the true palladium of liberty... The right of self-defense is the first law of nature; in most governments it has been the study of rulers to confine this right within the narrowest limits possible. Whenever standing armies are kept up, and the right of the people to keep and bear arms is, under any color or pretext whatsoever, prohibited, liberty, if not already annihilated, is on the brink of destruction. - St. George Tucker, Blackstone's Commentaries on the Laws of England (1803) (From which U.S. laws regarding the RKBA (The Human Right to Keep & Bear Arms) derived)

"Within the month, the convention had presented William and Mary with a Declaration of Rights that enumerated the ways in which James II had subverted the Constitution and the realm; listed thirteen rights and liberties of the people of England it characterized as "true, ancient and indubitable" that were to be recognized unequivocally; and elevated William and Mary to the throne as king and queen of England." - To Keep And Bear Arms by Dr. Joyce Malcolm

Fundamental, true ancient and indubitable human right. http://www.a-human-right.com/introduction.html

"I place economy among the first and most important of virtues, and public debt as the greatest of dangers to be feared." "To preserve our independence we must not let our leaders load us with perpetual debt. ....If we can prevent the government from wasting the labours of the people under the pretence of caring for them, we will be wise." - Thomas Jefferson, Author of the Declaration of Independence, 3rd President of the U.S.

"Allow a government to decline paying its debts and you overthrow all public morality--you unhinge all the principles that preserve the limits of free constitutions. Nothing can more affect national prosperity than a constant and systematic attention to extinguish the present debt and to avoid as much as possibly the incurring of any new debt." - Alexander Hamilton (1755-1804) Lawyer, Secretary of the Treasury & Secretary of State

"Still, if you will not fight for the right when you can easily win without bloodshed; if you will not fight when your victory will be sure and not too costly; you may come to the moment when you have to fight with all the odds against you and only a precarious chance of survival. There may even be a worse case. You may have to fight when there is no hope of victory, because it is better to perish than live as slaves." -Sir Winston Churchill

"Some regard private enterprise as if it were a predatory tiger to be shot. Others look upon it as a cow that they can milk. Only a handful see it for what it really is--the strong horse that pulls the whole cart." - Sir Winston Churchill

"Find out just what the people will submit to and you have found out the exact amount of injustice and wrong which will be imposed upon them; and these will continue until they are resisted with either words or blows, or with both. The limits of tyrants are prescribed by the endurance of those whom they oppress." - Frederick Douglass, Aug. 4, 1857

"Freedom is never voluntarily given by the oppressor; it must be demanded by the oppressed." – Martin Luther King, Jr.

"Ask yourself whether the dream of heaven and greatness should be waiting for us in our graves - or whether it should be ours here and now and on this earth." - Ayn Rand

"Do not let your fire go out, spark by irreplaceable spark, in the hopeless swamps of the approximate, the not-quite, the not-yet, the not-at-all. Do not let the hero in your soul perish, in lonely frustration for the life you deserved, but have never been able to reach. Check your road and the nature of your battle. The world you desired can be won, it exists, it is real, it is possible, it's yours." - "Atlas Shrugged", by Ayn Rand.

"The most valuable friends are not those who see you for what you are, but those who see you for what you can be." - Kira Saoirse, author of The Universal Individual Rights Project.

"Observe the character of our intellectual Establishment. It is about a hundred years behind the times. It holds as dogma the basic premises fashionable at the turn of the century: the mysticism of Kant, the collectivism of Marx, the altruism of street-corner evangelists. Two world wars, three monstrous dictatorships—in Soviet Russia, Nazi Germany, Red China—plus every lesser variant of devastating socialist experimentation in a global spread of brutality and despair, have not prompted modern intellectuals to question or revise their dogma. They still think that it is daring, idealistic and unconventional to denounce the rich.

They still believe that money is the root of all evil —except government money, which is the solution to all problems. The intellectual Establishment is frozen on the level of those elderly 'leaders' who were prominent when the system of governmental 'encouragement' took hold. By controlling the schools, the 'leaders' perpetuated their dogma and gradually silenced the opposition." - Ayn Rand, "Philosophy: Who Needs It", 1972.

www.ingramcontent.com/pod-product-compliance
Lightning Source LLC
Chambersburg PA
CBHW020542290526
45786CB00002B/991